MUSIC MINUS ONE FRENCH HORN

PACIFIC COAST HORNS

V O L U M E 3

Modern
FRENCH HORN
Flavors

3556

SUGGESTIONS FOR USING THIS MMO EDITION

WE HAVE TRIED to create a product that will provide you an easy way to learn and perform these compositions with a full ensemble in the comfort of your own home. The following MMO features and techniques will help you maximize the effectiveness of the MMO practice and performance system:

Because it involves a fixed accompaniment performance, there is an inherent lack of flexibility in tempo. We have observed generally accepted tempi, and always in the originally intended key, but some may wish to perform at a different tempo, or to slow down or speed up the accompaniment for practice purposes; or to alter the piece to a more comfortable key. For maximum flexibility, you can purchase from MMO specialized CD players & recorders which allow variable speed while maintaining proper pitch, and vice versa. This is an indispensable tool for the serious musician and you may wish to look into purchasing this useful piece of equipment for full enjoyment of all your MMO editions.

We want to provide you with the most useful practice and performance accompaniments possible. If you have any suggestions for improving the MMO system, please feel free to contact us. You can reach us by e-mail at *info@musicminusone.com*.

3556

CONTENTS

ISBN 978-1-59615-790-3

French horn

Alexander's Ragtime Band

By IRVING BERLIN
Arrangement by PAUL CHAUVIN

French horn

The Toy Trumpet

By RAYMOND SCOTT
transcribed by CHARLES WARREN

V. S.

MMO 3556

8

French horn

Stompin' at the Savoy

Words by Andy Razaf
Music by Benny Goodman, Edgar Sampson and Chick Webb
arrangement by Paul Chauvin

The Original, First and Foremost Version of:
The Blue Danube

French horn

the mistake waltz
by Johann Strauss, Jr.
arrangement by Paul Chauvin

French horn

Mysterious Mose

Words and Music by
WALTER DOYLE and TED WEEMS

Horn in F

Harlem Nocturne

Words by DICK ROGERS
Music by EARLE HAGEN
arrangement by PAUL CHAUVIN

French horn

Bugle Call Rag

by JACK PETTIS, BILLY MYERS
and ELMER SCHOEBEL
arrangement by CHARLES WARREN

French horn

Les Toreadors

from CARMEN

By GEORGE BIZET
arrangement by CHARLES WARREN

MMO 3556

Caravan
from SOPHISTICATED LADIES

Horn in F

Words and Music by
DUKE ELLINGTON, IRVING MILLS
and JUAN TIZOL
arrangement by PAUL CHAUVIN

French horn

Blue Rondo A La Turk

By DAVE BRUBECK
Arrangement by CHARLES WARREN

Horn in F

Amazing Grace

by JOHN NEWTON
arrangement by PAUL CHAUVIN

Horn in F

William Tell Overture

MMO 3556

MUSIC MINUS ONE
50 Executive Boulevard
Elmsford, New York 10523-1325
1.800.669.7464 (U.S.)/914.592.1188 (International)

www.musicminusone.com
e-mail: info@musicminusone.com